TRACK & FIELD

MIDDLE AND LONG DISTANCE RUNS

MORGAN HUGHES

The Rourke Press, Inc.
Vero Beach, Florida 32964

Morgan Hughes is a sports writer who has covered professional hockey, baseball, tennis and cycling. He has written several childrens books, both fiction and nonfiction, and is currently at work on his first full-length novel.

PROJECT ADVISOR:
Richard Roberts is the former head track and field coach at Florida State University, where he was also a star athlete during his undergraduate studies. He resides in Tallahassee with his wife and three hunting dogs.

PHOTO CREDITS:
All photos by Ryals Lee, Jr., except: ALLSPORT (pages 4, 18, 24, 39); Victah Sailer (pages 23, 26)

ILLUSTRATIONS:
Craig Werkheiser, Kingfish Studio (page 19)

EDITORIAL SERVICES: Janice L. Smith for Penworthy

Library of Congress Cataloging-in-Publication Data

Hughes, Morgan, 1957-
    Track and field / Morgan E. Hughes.
       p. cm.
    Include indexes.
    Contents: [1] An Introduction to Track & Field — [2] The sprints — [3] Middle and long distance runs — [4] The jumps — [5] The throws — [6] Training and fitness.
       ISBN 1-57103-288-6 (v. 1). — ISBN 1-57103-291-6 (v. 2). — ISBN 1-57103-289-4 (v. 3). — ISBN 1-57103-290-8 (v. 4). — ISBN 1-57103-292-4 (v. 5). — ISBN 1-57103-293-2 (v. 6)
    1. Track-athletics Juvenile literature. [1. Track and field.] I. Title.
GV1060.5.H833 1999
796.42—dc21   99-20284
                                                                    CIP

Printed in the USA

TABLE OF CONTENTS

Roger Bannister was the first man to break the four-minute mile barrier.

CHAPTER ONE

THE 1,500m & 3,000m RUNS

Ever since England's Roger Bannister became the first person to run a mile in less than four minutes in 1954, few track and field events have seen as much progress as distance running. From the mile (or 1,500-**meter**) run to the 26-mile, 385-yard (just under 42 kilometers) **marathon**, records have been set and broken with startling frequency.

Most track and field events require special equipment, such as something to throw or something to jump. Middle- and long-distance running takes only a good pair of shoes and willingness to work hard.

To succeed in distance running, a runner must work hard for years, building good health and fitness. Some people say, though, that distance running is as much a mental game as a physical one. The mind does play an important part in making the body perform at its best.

Teaching a special procedure for distance running is hard, especially for 1,500-meter and 3,000-meter runs. Each runner develops a method that works for him or her. Some basic actions, though, must be learned by beginners who hope to compete as distance runners.

The most important part of middle- and long-distance running is the stride. A proper stride helps prevent injuries—and failure.

The pelvic bone is key to getting the correct running posture. A runner's spine twists with each stride. As the pelvis moves forward and backward, it helps to control this twisting.

★ COACH'S CORNER

Medical experts agree that, along with staying away from drugs, alcohol, and tobacco, it is vital for all athletes—young and old, experienced and novice—to get enough sleep.

Long-distance runners take a more upright starting position.

Unlike sprinters, long-distance runners have a relaxed posture.

In shorter events, athletes run at the upper limit of their speed. In middle- and long-distance runs, though, runners work to maintain a steady pace that will sustain them for the entire race. A **kick** at the end of a race is important for middle- and long-distance runners. No matter the length of a running event, it is likely to end in a sprint with several runners hoping to use the last of their energy in a burst for the finish line. Distance runners often are not the best sprinters, so timing is important. A sprint to the finish must not start too soon. When another runner starts a final sprint, though, it's time for you to do the same.

As you run, keep your shoulders high, your back flat, and your chin up. Pretend that a straight line runs up from the ground through your upright torso. Hold your head at the top of this line, and always put your chest forward.

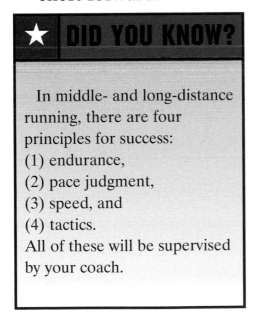

★ **DID YOU KNOW?**

In middle- and long-distance running, there are four principles for success:
(1) endurance,
(2) pace judgment,
(3) speed, and
(4) tactics.
All of these will be supervised by your coach.

With each step, bring up the heel of your launch foot until it almost hits you in the seat of your shorts. Try not to sway from side to side.

With your first stride, plant your foot flat. As your body comes forward over that foot, roll your weight to the inside and then forward off the ball of your foot, pushing off for the next step. Then repeat this procedure with your other foot, and so on with each stride.

Distance runners do not remain in their lanes for the entire race, but they do have individual starting positions.

Running in the "float" position requires lots of practice.

For a moment between foot plants, you will be in the "float position." The float position is as much a frame of mind as a physical posture. Your hands should be open and relaxed since making fists and swinging elbows wastes your energy. Your back should be flat and your forearms should be parallel to the ground.

To become a smooth, steady runner, think rhythm. Think coordination. Think relaxation.

Do you have a never-give-up attitude? Can you push yourself to do better in what you already do well? Do you like the tired-happy feeling that comes from running a l-o-n-g race? Can you handle stress? If so, you may have what it takes to be a distance runner.

THE 5,000m RUN & THE WALKS

For most boys and girls age 16 and younger, the longest running event will be a 3,000-meter run. Boys in the Young Adult (ages 17-18) group compete in a 5,000-meter run as well. Girls in the Young Adult group run a 3,000-meter race.

Young track athletes can race walk, starting with the 1,500-meter walk for Bantams (ages 10 and under) and Midgets (ages 11-12). Youth (ages 13-14), Intermediate (ages 15-16), and Young Adult athletes move up to a 3,000-meter walking race.

Running the Distance

A 5,000-meter run is about three miles and runners use many of the same techniques as 1,500-meter and 3,000-meter runners. Because of the longer distance, a runner needs more endurance for the 5,000-meter event. To build endurance, he or she will run more miles a week in training.

Many of the greatest 5,000-meter and 10,000-meter champions have been small in stature. For example, Pyotr Bolotnikov, the 1960 Summer Olympic 10,000-meter champion (USSR), stood 5 feet, 8 inches (1.72 meters). The 5,000- and 10,000-meter events are ideal for athletes who lack the body build for other events but who are willing to train hard.

Body position is as important in these longer races as in the 1,500- and 3,000-meter runs. Pacing to save energy is important, too. One of the most important things for a young distance runner to do is to stay in contact with other groups of runners during a race. Covering a great distance—often under less than ideal conditions—is hard. Running alone behind the rest of the pack is harder.

DID YOU KNOW?

In the 1970s, American "golden boy" Steve Prefontaine was virtually unbeatable in the 5,000 meters until a car accident ruined his chances for Olympic gold medal glory.

Long-distance runners may share a lane.

It's important to listen to your coach.

A 5,000-meter specialist runs many miles to prepare for races. Many of these miles are run during **interval training** (400m, 800m, and 1,500m distances). **Free running**, though, makes up most of the training for a 5,000-meter runner.

Distance running takes patience and belief in your ability to finish the race. Sometimes, especially in young athletes, a lack of confidence spoils an event before it begins.

The brain sends messages about fatigue and discomfort long before the body is ready to quit. While running, you may feel that you cannot take another step. Really, though, you may have plenty of gas left in your tank.

So you need to know yourself. Work with your coach to find your limits. All runners experience some discomfort and fatigue. Learn to put them out of your mind.

★ **DID YOU KNOW?**

"Fartlek" training is similar to interval training. It involves mixing bursts of speed (sprints) during slower running (jogging) to help develop speed. These intervals can be tailored to each athlete.

Walking the Distance

Some people think race walking is for boys and girls (or men and women) who do not have the speed or strength for standard track and field events. Many of the world's best race walkers are also good all-around athletes, however.

Race walking is very technical.

Though it may look "odd," race walking is very competitive.

You may not think of walking as a sport because you do it every day without thinking about it. In a walking race, though, walkers must follow rigid rules. For example, a race walker must have some part of one foot on the ground at all times. Mastering the **heel-toe** step, in which the heel of the walker's front foot touches the ground before the toes of the rear foot are lifted from the ground, is essential for race walkers.

Race walkers also must learn a hip-swing action that makes their strides longer, without breaking the heel-toe step. Style and method are much more important than speed to a novice race walker. Speed comes after good techniques are in place—partly because of them.

THE MARATHON

From Boston and New York to San Francisco, and from Chicago to Tallahassee, marathons attract racers the world over. So the marathon came to be called the glamour event of track and field.

The marathon, like other middle- and long-distance runs, is a simple event. Its main requirement is a love of running. A marathon runner must be at the peak of his or her fitness. For marathoners, fitness and endurance are more important than speed. Most important of all are rhythm in the stride and a relaxed running style. Both of these qualities come from steady training.

The marathon is a road race, not a track race. Even in the Olympics, where it starts and finishes on a stadium track, most of the marathon is run on a road, or cross-country, course.

To prepare for this extra-long event, a runner works out his or her own training schedule and method. What works well for one runner may not work at all for another.

No special equipment is needed for cross-country runs. To train, most marathoners use interval training on an oval track. Training on a track helps runners build the speed needed at the end of a race.

★ DID YOU KNOW?

The first marathon of the modern Olympic era was held in Athens in 1896. Nowadays, there are important marathons held in many major international cities every year.

Marathons may start and finish in a stadium, but they're run on roadways.

The "shuffle" step helps marathoners avoid leg injuries.

The marathon is harder than any other track event on a runner's feet, ankles, knees, hips, and back. The rock-solid surface they run on is the cause. For this reason, marathoners do not use the body-jarring high step of runners in other events. Instead they use a **"shuffle" step**, in which their feet remain close to the ground.

Also, the length of a marathon causes tired, sore muscles. Runners in short, fast events suffer **oxygen debt**. That is, the oxygen in their blood dips low. For marathon runners, though, muscle pain is more of a problem than oxygen debt. In fact, a marathoner is rarely out of breath at the end of a race. Exhaustion is common, though. To help with fatigue, many marathoners use over-distance training. That is, they run more than 26 miles (about 42 kilometers)—say, up to 30 miles (48 kilometers) at a time.

★ **DID YOU KNOW?**

The marathon gets its name from a tale of an ancient Greek messenger who ran from the village of Marathon to Athens with a message about the war with the Persians, then dropped dead.

A marathon is not won at the beginning but in the last eight to ten miles (12 to 16 kilometers). Fast starts are foolish. The goal of a long-distance runner should be consistency. A consistent runner runs the same every time he or she trains or runs a race. Do you think you have a marathon in you? If so, be consistent in your stride. Be consistent in your breathing. Be consistent in your attitude and style, too. Most of all, be consistent in your training.

It's important to stay relaxed and focused during a long run.

THE STEEPLECHASE

One of the most demanding tests for all runners is the steeplechase, which is run on a regulation stadium track. The basic difference between the steeplechase and such races as the 3,000-, 5,000- and 10,000-meter runs is the addition of hurdles—one of which is a potentially hazardous water jump. The steeplechase is comprised of several laps around the track, with the hurdles (heavy track-wide obstacles, not the lightweight single-lane hurdles) placed in the turns. This grueling race may not be for everyone. However, for the brave runner who tries, it can be rewarding.

The steeplechase combines distance running and hurdling.

Most coaches suggest five 15-mile (24-kilometer) training runs a week for marathoners. Training runs are somewhat slower than race speed. Marathon runners also need exercises to stretch and strengthen muscles.

As a budding middle- and long-distance runner, you are probably still years away from trying your first marathon. By the time you do, you will have had lots of experience in 1,500-meter and 3,000-meter runs, and perhaps even 5,000-meter and 10,000-meter events. A marathon is truly a long-distance run! Be sure you are ready before you take it on.

THE DECATHLON

No greater test of all-around athletic ability exists than the **decathlon**. The word comes from the Greek words *deka* (ten) and *athos* (contest or struggle).

This two-day event for male athletes 15 years or older is a combination of ten track and field events: (1) 100-meter sprint, (2) 400-meter sprint, (3) 1,500-meter run, (4) 110-meter **hurdles,** (5) long jump, (6) high jump, (7) discus throw, (8) javelin throw, (9) pole vault, and (10) **shot put**.

Younger athletes compete in the **triathlon** (three events) and **pentathlon** (five events).

As if these events were not difficult enough, a decathlete must compete in five events on the first day and then perform the other five events the very next day. Because of its rugged schedule, many experts consider the decathlon the most difficult track and field contest.

The built-in challenge of this demanding trial is its variety. A decathlete must be able to do a lot of different things very well. He must add the grace of a high jumper to the strength of a shot-putter. A decathlete must have the explosive speed of a sprinter and the stamina of a miler, too.

★ **DID YOU KNOW?**

Since its inception in 1904, American men have won 11 of 20 Olympic gold medals in the decathlon—most recently Dan O'Brien in 1996. No other nation has more than two.

The decathlon includes many events and many different implements.

It takes strength and agility to succeed in pole vaulting.

A champion in this event is a very special athlete who must be committed to training. He must be willing to work long hours on different skills and deal with fatigue and frustration to master them all. A poor performance in just one of the ten events can ruin a decathlete's overall score.

The decathlete must be an excellent all-around athlete, with great coordination, speed, and strength. Young men with the muscles for football, the speed and coordination for baseball, and the grace and stamina for basketball may have what the decathlon takes.

Of all the physical traits needed for the decathlon, endurance is the least important. The only long event is a 1,500-meter run. This event is usually the last one on the second day, so the resulting fatigue does not interfere with the other contests.

★ **DID YOU KNOW?**

Before he took the world by storm in 1976, Olympic decathlon gold medalist Bruce Jenner was enrolled at Graceland College, a Mormon school in Iowa, where he was on a football scholarship.

Up-and-coming decathletes face other problems. The number and variety of events means the risk of injury is greater than it would be for the one-event athlete. While most track and field athletes have only one coach to look to for advice, a decathlete may have up to ten coaches—one for each event.

Spending time in the weight room is a good idea.

Decathletes must work on speed for the sprint events.

A decathlete must prepare well for each event. He may warm up for a 100-meter sprint in a different way than he does for a javelin throw. With so many events to train for, most decathletes practice several of them during a training session.

Being a decathlon threat takes more than being pretty good in a lot of events. An athlete has to excel in at least seven of the ten events if he wants to win a decathlon title today.

Would you like to get started in this exciting sport? Don't be put off by the huge challenge. You do not have to be a world-class sprinter, a record-setting shot-putter, or a top-ten high jumper. The most important skills you have are your all-around ability and your desire to work hard.

CHAPTER FIVE

TRIATHLON, PENTATHLON & HEPTATHLON

Women have gone far in track and field in recent years. Much progress has been made in the **heptathlon**, a tough seven-event challenge. For women competing at the 1984 Olympic games, the heptathlon replaced the pentathlon.

Before an athlete competes in the heptathlon at the Intermediate level, she tests her skills in the Bantam triathlon. Then she goes on to the pentathlon for Midget and Youth.

The original pentathlon in ancient Greece consisted of a run, the long jump, discus, javelin, and wrestling. When the modern Olympics began (1896), the men's pentathlon involved different events: the 200-meter run, the 1,500-meter run, discus, javelin, and long jump.

The men's pentathlon was discontinued after the 1924 Olympics, but the event resumed in 1954. Ten years later, when women began competing in the pentathlon, Irina Press of the Soviet Union won the gold medal. At the 1984 Summer Olympics, the heptathlon replaced the pentathlon for women.

Then, at the 1988 Summer Games in Seoul, South Korea, Jackie Joyner-Kersee (U.S.) set a world record in the heptathlon. She won the long jump, too, setting a new Olympic record of 24 feet, 3 ½ inches (7.4 meters).

★ **DID YOU KNOW?**

Named for former First Lady Jacqueline Kennedy, heptathlete Jackie Joyner-Kersee won two consecutive Olympic gold medals—in 1988, when she set the Olympic record with 7,291 points, and in 1992.

Jackie Joyner-Kersee is the greatest woman heptathlete in Olympic history.

CHANGES IN MULTIPLE EVENTS

BANTAM (10 & UNDER) TRIATHLON	BOYS	GIRLS
	6-lb. shot put	6-lb. shot put
	high jump	high jump
	400-meter run	200-meter run

MIDGET (11-12) PENTATHLON	BOYS	GIRLS
	6-lb. shot put	6-lb. shot put
	high jump	high jump
	long jump	long jump
	80-meter hurdles	80-meter hurdles
	1,500-meter run	800-meter run

YOUTH (13-14) PENTATHLON	BOYS	GIRLS
	4-kg. shot put (8.8 lbs.)	6-lb. shot put
	high jump	high jump
	long jump	long jump
	100-meter hurdles	80-meter hurdles
	1,500-meter run	800-meter run

INTERMEDIATE (15-16) & YOUNG ADULT (17-18)		BOYS DECATHLON	GIRLS HEPTATHLON
	Day 1	100-meter run	100-meter hurdles
		long jump	high jump
		4-kg. shot put (8.8 lbs.)	6-lb. shot put
		high jump	200-meter run
		1,500 meter run	
	Day 2	110-meter hurdles	long jump
		discus	javelin
		pole vault	800-meter run
		javelin	
		1,500-meter run	

With the addition of events, the triathlon and pentathlon eventually become the decathlon (boys) and the heptathlon (girls).

The Bantam triathlon consists of the shot put, high jump, and 200-meter run (girls) or 400-meter run (boys). Girls and boys in the Midget and Youth groups compete in the pentathlon. While boys go on to the decathlon as Intermediates, girls move up to the heptathlon.

The USA Track and Field (USATF) pentathlon for Midget girls now includes 80-meter hurdles, six-pound shot put, high jump, long jump, and the 800-meter run. Moving up an age group brings a bigger challenge. For example, boys in the Youth level (ages 13-14) go from 80-meter hurdles (as Midgets) to 100-meter hurdles.

A different set of events face young women in the Young Adult (ages 17-18) heptathlon: six-pound shot put, 200- and 800-meter run, high jump, javelin throw, 100-meter hurdles, and long jump.

★ DID YOU KNOW?

Shirley Strickland of Australia was the first woman to win gold medals in successive Olympic Games (1952 and 1956), capturing her second 80-meter hurdles medal in Melbourne.

A heptathlete must have many strengths and abilities. Before Jackie Joyner-Kersee won Olympic gold medals (1988 and 1992) in the heptathlon, she played college basketball at UCLA and excelled in the long jump on the track team. When her basketball coach, Bob Kersee (her future husband), saw her great versatility, he convinced her to begin training for the heptathlon.

OLYMPIC CHAMPIONS

PENTATHLON

1964	Irina Press, USSR	5246 points, World Record
1968	Ingrid Becker, West Germany	5098 points
1972	Mary Peters, Great Britain	4801 points, World Record*
1976	Siegrun Siegl, East Germany	4745 points
1980	Nadezhada Tkachenko, USSR	5083 points

HEPTATHLON

1984	Glynis Nunn, Australia	6390 points, World Record
1988	Jackie Joyner-Kersee, USA	7291 points, World Record
1992	Jackie Joyner-Kersee, USA	7044 points
1996	Ghada Shouaa, Syria	6780 points

*In 1971, 100-meter hurdles replaced 80-meter hurdles, bringing a change in scoring tables.

Jackie Joyner-Kersee is the only woman to win two Olympic gold medals in the heptathlon.

Hopping the short hurdles builds strength and stamina.

Joyner-Kersee dominated the 1988 Summer Games, destroying the field in the heptathlon on her way to an Olympic and world record for total points (7,291).

A heptathlete needs rare overall ability and the willingness to work on many skills at once. If you are looking to compete in the heptathlon, train for well-rounded fitness. You will need grace and quickness for the hurdling events. You also will need power and balance for the throwing events (shot put and javelin). To top off these skills, you will need the abilities of a 3,000-meter runner. The more you train for overall fitness, the better you will do.

GLOSSARY

decathlon (di KATH lahn) — a test for male athletes that includes ten track and field events to be completed over two days

free running (FREE RUN ing) — running on a road instead of a track; cross-country running

heel-toe (HEEL TO) — procedure used in race walking in which some part of the foot must be in contact with the ground at all times

heptathlon (hep TATH lahn) — a test for female athletes that includes seven track and field events to be completed over two days

hurdles (HERD lz) — horizontal bars the width of a lane on a track, held by upright posts and raised to various heights, which must be jumped by athletes in a sprint race

interval training (INT er vul TRAYN ing) — short, medium, and long runs use in training for long-distance races

kick (KIK) — the sprint at the end of a long-distance race

marathon (MAIR uh THAHN) — a road race of 26 miles, 385 yards (just under 42 kilometers)

GLOSSARY

meter (MEET er) — a unit of measurement in the metric system used in international competition to measure distances in races and throws; a meter is just over a yard (39.37 inches versus 36 inches). The 1,500-meter race is called the metric mile because it is closest in length (1,640 yards) to a mile (1,760 yards)

oxygen debt (AHK seh jen DET) — a condition of too little oxygen in the blood system, a problem of short-distance sprinters more than long-distance runners

pentathlon (pen TATH lahn) — a test that includes five track and field events that must be completed by an athlete in one day

shuffle step (SHUH fl STEP) — a technique used by marathon runners to protect their feet, ankles, knees, hips, and back from shock

shot put (SHAHT PUT) — an event in which a heavy steel ball (the shot) is thrown (or put) for distance

triathlon (tri ATH lahn) — a junior track and field event that includes running, jumping, and shot-putting. (An adult event by the same name includes running, biking, and swimming.)

FURTHER READING

Find out more with these helpful books and information sites:

Bowerman, William J. and Freeman, William H. *High Performance Training for Track and Field,* Human Kinetics, 1990

Carr, Gerry A. *Fundamentals of Track and Field,* Human Kinetics, 1991

Koch, Edward R. *USA Track and Field Directory,* USATF, 1993

Santos, Jim and Shannon, Ken. *Sports Illustrated Track,* S.I. 1991

American Track and Field Online
    at www.runningnetwork.com/aft/

M-F Athletic Company at
    www.mfathletic.com (an online catalog for track and field books,
    tapes, clothes, etc.)

Track and Field News at
    www.trackandfieldnews.com/

United States of America Track and Field at
    www.usatf.org

INDEX